D1520302

THIS BOOK BELONGS TO:

A CURIOUS BOY NAMED Jeff

Little Kids' Big Lessons

A CURIOUS BOY NAMED Jeff

Based on Jeff Bezos's life

Written By: Kay B

Meet Jeff.
He was a very curious boy.
He wanted to know how
things worked and why.

He would ask lots
of questions.
Asking questions is
a great way to learn.

Jeff enjoyed learning new
lessons in school,
especially about
math and science.

He paid attention and listened
carefully to his teachers.

Jeff also liked reading.
He read many kinds of books.
His favorite kind was science fiction.

Reading gives you tons
of knowledge
and helps grow
your imagination.

When Jeff wasn't reading, he spent time experimenting.

Experimenting means trying new ways of doing things.

Jeff's experiments helped him to create his own machines like a gate opener and an alarm for his bedroom.

Jeff loved spending time with his
grandfather the most.

He would watch his grandfather
work on his ranch
and help him out too.

Jeff learned how to fix broken tools
and build a house from scratch.

Observing and helping others helps
you to learn new skills.

As Jeff got older, he became curious about the computer and internet.

The internet helps people find information on anything and everything.

Jeff learned that he could
use them to help people and started
his own company called Amazon.

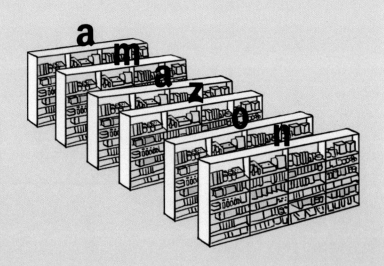

Amazon helps people
buy and sell anything using
the computer and internet.

You can buy toys,
books and even groceries.

Jeff wants to keep helping
people and everyday
he is trying to find
ways to do that.

He keeps asking questions,
observes the people around him,
and continues to read
and experiment.

If you do the same, maybe one day you will discover something new and can change the world too.

About the Author

Kay B was born in Queens, New York and currently lives in Seattle, Washington with her husband and son. She works full-time and has a career in Finance. Always fond of reading books herself, she enjoys reading stories to her son. She especially loves stories that teach kids morals. With this first-time, self-published children's book, Kay B hopes to share an important lesson on being curious, which she believes will help kids to learn and grow.

About the Illustrator

Adriana was born in Colombia, she enjoys painting and
drawing since was a little girl,
she married someone who enjoy art too,
she works alongside her husband indeed,
she works and has raised
two children, a boy and a girl.
They have worked together for the last 10 years,
almost exclusively in editorial projects for children's
and youth books.
They has published more than 50 books.
She likes photography, sow and care for plants, walk
her beagle and spend time with her family.

Manufactured by Amazon.ca
Bolton, ON